Ireland

Donna Bailey and Anna Sproule

STECK-VAUGHN
L I B R A R Y
A Division of Steck-Vaughn Company

Hello! My name is Niall and this is my family.

My brother Kevin is holding our collie.

Mary and Kathleen are my two sisters.

My little brother Brian is in front of Uncle Seamus.

Grandma's sitting on a chair.

2

We live in Ireland.
My Dad is a farmer and our farm is in
Kerry County in southwest Ireland.

Here, it rains most of the time.
The rain makes the grass grow,
and the country always looks green.
That's why some people call Ireland
the Emerald Isle.

Dad grows wheat and potatoes on the farm.
Irish people enjoy eating potatoes with
their meals.

Like everyone else, Grandpa helps Dad on the farm.
Grandma gets very angry with Grandpa
when he comes into the house and
forgets to take his boots off!

Mom keeps chickens in the yard.

The chickens give us all the eggs we need.

Mom sells the extra eggs in the village.

The cows on the farm eat the green grass
and give us lots of milk.
We have so many cows that we milk them by machine.
The cows in this picture are going into
the milking barn.

Inside the milking barn, Dad fits tubes
to the cows.
The tubes take the milk from the cows' udders.
Dad plays music for the cows.
The cows stand still and listen to the music
while they are being milked!

We pour the milk into milk cans and
I help deliver some of the milk to the village.
Dad takes the rest of the milk to the dairy
where it is made into butter and cream.

Once a month Dad chooses some cows to sell.
He herds the cows down the road to our farm.
Then he loads the cows into a truck and
takes them to the cattle market in
the nearest town.

11

On market days, cattle often
roam around the streets while
their owners go shopping.

At the cattle market,

the farmers put their cows into pens.

Then the farmers take turns selling their cows.

The cows are auctioned off one at a time.

Each cow is led into the pen.

The auctioneer starts the bidding for that cow.

The farmers bid what they'll pay for the cow.

The farmer who bids the most money buys the cow.

Grandpa has a few sheep in the hills
near the farm.
He keeps the sheep for their meat
and their wool.

Grandpa sells the wool to weavers.

Irish weavers make carpets and a cloth called tweed.

People buy tweed to make skirts and jackets.

Every year, Grandpa goes to the sheep fair in Dingle.
He takes along some sheep he wants to sell
and finds new sheep he wants to buy.
Grandpa meets his friends there, too.

People in Ireland love horses.

Many farmers raise horses for people to ride.

A favorite Irish vacation is to stay

at a farm and go trail-riding.

Farmers buy and sell horses at
horse fairs like this one at Connemara.
There are many horse fairs
in southwest Ireland.

The farmers lead their horses around the ring.
The judges look at the horses carefully
and decide which horse is the best.

At this horse fair in Dingle the farmer
is looking at the horse's legs to make sure
they are strong and healthy.
He wants to train the horse to race.

With so many horses and fairs
there is always plenty of work for
the blacksmith.

Sometimes the farmer sells a mare
and her foal together at a fair.
The buyer hopes the foal will win prizes
at the Royal Dublin Show when it is older.

The Royal Dublin Show is the biggest
horse show of the year in Ireland.
It takes place during a week in August.
Riders come from all over the world
to take part in the show-jumping events.

The show is very popular.
Crowds of people watch
all the different events.

Before the show starts, the band plays
Irish tunes and marches around the arena.

Teams of riders compete in
the different races to win prizes.
This is a relay race where each rider
must pick up a ball from the bucket.

In addition to jumping competitions and races,
there are other events during the show.
This picture shows a competition to find
the best cart horse.

This is a competition to find
the best horse in the show.
The owners parade their horses
in the ring, and the judges decide
which one will be the horse of the year.

The main show-jumping event is
the competition for the Aga Khan Cup.
The owner of the winning horse gets
a gold cup and lots of money.

The riders parade in front
of the grandstand.
Pipers playing bagpipes walk in front
of the horses and the crowd claps and cheers.

Behind the grandstand there are
lots of other things for people to do.
You can even have your face painted
to look like a clown!

Index

Reading Consultant: Diana Bentley
Editorial Consultant: Donna Bailey
Executive Editor: Elizabeth Strauss
Project Editor: Becky Ward

Picture research by Jennifer Garratt
Designed by Richard Garratt Design

Photographs
Cover: © Geoff Dore / TSW-Click / Chicago
Colorific Photo Library: 5 (Martin Rogers), 16 (Ronny Jaques), 17,21 (Linda Bartlett)
Robert Harding Picture Library: 2,14,15,19,20,23 (Desmond Harney)
Royal Dublin Society: 24,25,26,27,28,29,30,31,32
The Slide File: 3,7,8,11,13,22
The Telegraph Colour Library: 6 (D. Kasterine), 9 (Ian Murphy)
Tony Stone Worldwide: title page, 4,10,12,18

Library of Congress Cataloging-in-Publication Data: Bailey, Donna. Ireland / Donna Bailey and Anna Sproule.
p. cm.—(Where we live) Summary: A child living on a farm in County Kerry describes everyday life, market
day, a horse fair in Dingle, and the biggest horse show in Ireland, the Royal Dublin Show. ISBN
0-8114-2562-2 I. Kerry (Ireland)—Social life and customs—Juvenile literature. 2. Farm life—Ireland—Kerry—
Juvenile literature. 3. Horse-shows-Ireland—Juvenile literature. [1. Ireland—Social life and customs.] I. Sproule,
Anna. II. Title. III. Series: Bailey, Donna. Where we live. DA990.K4B35 1990 941.9′6—dc20 90-9645
CIP AC